Original title:
Finding My Heart

Copyright © 2024 Swan Charm
All rights reserved.

Author: Daisy Dewi
ISBN HARDBACK: 978-9916-89-927-4
ISBN PAPERBACK: 978-9916-89-928-1
ISBN EBOOK: 978-9916-89-929-8

Heartstrings of the Universe

In the silence of the night,
Stars whisper ancient truths.
Guided by a holy light,
We tread on sacred paths.

The sun breaks with gentle grace,
Painting skies with warmth divine.
Time weaves its tranquil lace,
Binding hearts with love's design.

Every heartbeat echoes wide,
As the cosmos sings our name.
In this vastness, we abide,
Connected, yet all the same.

Grains of sand, each one unique,
Form the shores of endless seas.
In our spirits, hope will speak,
Sowing faith like gentle breeze.

Beyond the veil of our eyes,
Lives a melody so grand.
In each tear and every sigh,
Is the touch of God's own hand.

Embracing the Infinite Call

In the stillness, voices rise,
Calling forth the souls in need.
Heaven's grace, a soft reprise,
Gives us strength, in faith, we lead.

Mountains bow, and rivers weep,
Nature's choir sings the hymn.
In our hearts, the secrets seep,
Of the light that never dims.

Beneath the stars, we gather close,
In unity, our spirits soar.
Through the trials, we are morose,
Yet, find solace evermore.

Hands extended, love's embrace,
Breaking chains that bind us here.
In the shadows, we find grace,
As we chase away our fear.

Journey forth, the path is clear,
Boundless love, our guiding flame.
With each step, we persevere,
In His name, we call the same.

The Altar of Vulnerability

On this altar, spirits bare,
Truths come forth without pretense.
In our pain, we learn to care,
Finding beauty in the tense.

Hearts laid open like the sky,
Fears dissolve in light's embrace.
Courage blooms as we comply,
With the love we dare to face.

In our frailty, strength we find,
Shattered pieces form a whole.
Every wound becomes aligned,
Healing comes to free our soul.

Each confession, a sweet grace,
Binding ties that knew no end.
In the depths, we find our place,
Where the broken hearts can mend.

Through this journey, hand in hand,
We discover who we are.
In our flaws, a quiet stand,
Leads us gently to the star.

When Faith Becomes Flesh

In the morning's gentle light,
Hope unfurls like petals wide.
Faith transcends the dark of night,
Carving paths where shadows hide.

Each kind word becomes our deed,
Living out the love we seek.
In our hearts, we plant the seed,
Nurturing the spirit weak.

With every breath, we're reborn,
Finding grace in daily strife.
In our silence, we are sworn,
To embrace the gift of life.

When we walk in humble trust,
Every step becomes a prayer.
Turning doubt to holy dust,
Guided by the love we share.

Faith in action, hands that reach,
Show the world a brighter way.
In our lives, His lessons teach,
When faith is flesh, we are His sway.

The Refuge of Kindred Spirits

In the garden of souls, we meet,
Where hearts align, and spirits greet.
A bond unbroken, woven tight,
In shared whispers, we find our light.

Through trials faced, we stand as one,
Guided by stars, beneath the sun.
In laughter, tears, our spirits soar,
Together we heal, forevermore.

Each gentle touch, a sacred gift,
In kindness pure, our spirits lift.
A refuge found in sacred grace,
In love's embrace, we find our place.

The echoes of our laughter ring,
As nature sings, the joy we bring.
In moments shared, the world's so wide,
With kindred spirits, we abide.

Together we walk this sacred path,
In every storm, we find the math.
With hearts united, we ascend,
In love's embrace, we never end.

A Pilgrimage of Love and Light

On winding roads, our journey grows,
With every step, the spirit knows.
Through valleys low and mountains high,
We seek the truth, beneath the sky.

In every heart, a flame ignites,
A beacon shining in the nights.
Together bound, we rise and roam,
In love and light, we find our home.

With every prayer, our voices blend,
In harmony, we learn to mend.
Through trials faced, our strength is found,
In sacred love, we stand our ground.

The stars above, a guiding hand,
With faith, we walk this hallowed land.
Each moment shared, a gem so rare,
In pilgrimage, we breathe the air.

For love leads brave hearts to the shore,
Where kindness flows forevermore.
With every heartbeat, we unite,
On this pilgrimage of love and light.

The Story Written on My Heart

In every line, a tale unfolds,
A whispered truth that gently holds.
In shadows cast, the light shall gleam,
For every sorrow births a dream.

With ink of hope and tears of grace,
The story flows, a sacred space.
In every heartbeat, chapters bloom,
In love's embrace, dispelling gloom.

Past wounds shall heal with tender care,
As we're reminded, love is rare.
Each moment penned, a treasure dear,
The story written, crystal clear.

In laughter shared and lessons learned,\nThrough paths of light, our spirits yearned.
In every sigh, a sacred spark,
Illuminates the journey's arc.

And when the pages start to fade,
With every shadow, joy's remade.
For on my heart, the truth resides,
The story lives, in love abides.

Sacred Symbols of True Connection

In symbols drawn, our hearts align,
With every mark, a truth divine.
In quiet moments, spirits speak,
The warmth we share is what we seek.

A glance exchanged, a knowing smile,
In sacred bonds, we walk the mile.
Each touch, a whisper from the soul,
In unity, we are made whole.

The threads of love bind us so tight,
In every dark, we find the light.
With open hearts, we share the way,
In sacred symbols, we hold sway.

Through trials faced and moments shared,\nIn love's embrace, we are prepared.
The signs of hope, a guiding beam,
In true connection, we dare to dream.

So raise your heart and open wide,
In sacred symbols, love's our guide.
Together we journey, hand in hand,
In this connection, we understand.

In the Garden of Grace

In the garden where flowers bloom,
The light dances, dispelling gloom.
Whispers of faith in every breeze,
In this haven, the soul finds ease.

Beneath the arch of gentle skies,
The heart awakens, love never dies.
Tread softly on this sacred ground,
Where heaven's serenade is found.

Each petal a prayer, each leaf a dream,
In life's tapestry, we weave and seam.
With hands uplifted to the divine,
In the garden, our spirits align.

In shadows deep, the light still shines,
Guiding us through the trials of time.
With every breath, our souls declare,
In the garden of grace, love is our prayer.

Soliloquy of Spirit and Heart

In silence deep, my spirit sings,
A symphony of unseen things.
Words unspoken, yet deeply felt,
In the heart, where emotions melt.

Each pulse a sonnet, each sigh a verse,
In the dance of life, we immerse.
With open arms, we embrace the light,
In the shadows, finding our sight.

Awake, O spirit, rise from slumber,
In the heart's echoes, seek the wonder.
A soliloquy of love and grace,
In every tear, His warm embrace.

We walk this path, hand in hand,
Guided by faith, together we stand.
With every heartbeat, the truth we find,
A symphony sweet, in souls intertwined.

Celestial Echoes of Belonging

In the stillness of the night,
Stars whisper secrets, pure delight.
Each twinkle a reminder clear,
We are loved, forever near.

Voices rising, a sacred choir,
Singing praises, lifting higher.
In celestial light, we are one,
The journey of souls just begun.

Bound by grace, through trials we go,
In unity, our spirits grow.
With every heartbeat, echoes call,
In the dance of life, we rise, we fall.

Embrace the light, let shadows flee,
In belonging, we find the key.
Together we stand in faith's strong arms,
Eternal echoes, love's sweet charms.

The Pilgrim's Prayer for Wholeness

O Lord, I wander on this path,
Seeking the light, escaping wrath.
In every step, a prayer I hold,
For wholeness in heart, for stories untold.

Through valleys low and mountains high,
With faith as my guide, I seek the sky.
Each moment a gift, each breath a chance,
In the dance of life, I take my stance.

With sorrow and joy, I journey on,
In humility's light, all burdens gone.
O gentle spirit, grant me grace,
In the essence of love, I find my place.

Unlock the chains that hold me near,
With every echo, I draw you near.
In this pilgrimage, my heart unfolds,
In oneness with You, my soul beholds.

The Parable of the Restless Heart

In shadows deep the heart does roam,
Seeking peace, a distant home.
Yet in the void, a whisper calls,
To trust the light that never falls.

With every sigh the spirit yearns,
To find the tide that ever churns.
Through trials faced and tempests braved,
Awake the love that once was saved.

The restless heart finds rest in grace,
When faith reflects a warm embrace.
A journey led by truth, not fear,
Will light the path and draw us near.

Let not despair take hold of thee,
For every falling leaf can see.
That in the cycle of the night,
There dawns a hope, a radiant light.

In every struggle, find the key,
A lesson learned, a glimpse set free.
The parable of love unfolds,
In every heart, a tale retold.

Emissaries of Love in Motion

From every corner, voices rise,
With gentle words, beneath the skies.
Emissaries cloaked in grace,
They bear the light to every place.

With open hands and lifted hearts,
They weave the hope that never parts.
To every soul in shadows cast,
Love's tender touch will ever last.

Together we become the flame,
In unity, we share one name.
Moving forward, step by step,
In every tear, a promise kept.

As rivers flow, our spirits blend,
In loving kindness, hearts extend.
A tapestry of souls entwined,
In love's embrace, we seek and find.

Let every action, pure and true,
Reflect the light that shines anew.
Emissaries, brave and bold,
In every heart, a truth retold.

Sunbeams through the Clouds of Doubt

When shadows creep, and doubts arise,
Through heavy clouds there pierce the skies.
Sunbeams glisten on the way,
To guide the heart, to light the day.

In whispers soft the truth shall speak,
A promise strong for those who seek.
In darkest nights, hope's ember glows,
With every breath, a vision grows.

Each trial faced, a lesson learned,
From ashes rise the fires burned.
For strength is found in fragile places,
Where love awakens warm embraces.

Through storms we brave, through winds we sail,
In unity, we shall prevail.
For every doubt that clouds the heart,
The sun will rise, a brand new start.

Let faith ignite the dawn anew,
To see the skies in vibrant hue.
Sunbeams shining through the night,
Will guide us toward the sacred light.

The Canvas of Celestial Longing

Upon the canvas of the soul,
Each stroke of faith makes us whole.
Celestial dreams in colors bright,
Awakening hearts to pure delight.

With every yearning, brush in hand,
We paint the sky, we take our stand.
In every hue, a story flows,
Of love that grows as spirit glows.

The stars above, they call our name,
In whispers soft, we feel the flame.
A longing deep for realms divine,
In every heartbeat, we align.

As artists of the heart, we strive,
To craft a world where love can thrive.
Each tender stroke a prayer, a plea,
To fill the void with harmony.

Let every moment shape the art,
A masterpiece from each kind heart.
The canvas vast, love's colors blend,
In celestial longing, we ascend.

The Heart's Nebula of Hope

In the stillness of the night,
Stars whisper soft and bright,
Dreams woven on threads of light,
Guiding souls to realms of right.

Each heartbeat sings a prayer,
Lifted high in gentle air,
Hope like petals, pure and rare,
Blooming kindly, everywhere.

Through valleys deep and shadows long,
The spirit raises its sweet song,
In the dance of life, where we belong,
We find the strength to carry on.

With faith as fierce as summer sun,
In every challenge, we are one,
Together bound, our journey spun,
In love's embrace, we've just begun.

A nebula where dreams ignite,
Hearts aglow with sacred light,
In unity, our visions sight,
Hope forever, burning bright.

Celestial Caresses on My Journey

Soft whispers from the sky,
Angels singing lullabies,
Guiding me where I must fly,
In the arms of love, I sigh.

Each step I take, a gentle grace,
Touched by light, I find my place,
Through every trial, in every space,
Heaven's hand I embrace.

Stars twinkle like distant kin,
Guardian spirits, deep within,
Leading me through loss and sin,
In their warmth, my soul can win.

Miracles unfold in time,
Whispers gentle, voices chime,
As I walk pathways divine,
The universe, a sacred rhyme.

On this journey, love's the key,
In its light, I feel so free,
Celestial caresses, guiding me,
In eternal peace, I'll be.

Sacred Echoes of the Soul's Yearning

In the silence of my heart,
A longing sings, a work of art,
Whispers of the soul impart,
Sacred truths that never part.

Echoes of the ancient call,
Through the stillness, I stand tall,
In every rise, in every fall,
Spirit's song, a timeless thrall.

Yearnings like the river flow,
Carving paths where love will grow,
In the sacred, soft aglow,
Guided by what we both know.

Each moment shares a spark divine,
Connecting threads of yours and mine,
In the dance of fate, we shine,
Life's a sacred, grand design.

Through the struggles, I will seek,
In every truth, in every peak,
With faith that whispers, ever meek,
The soul's yearning, bold yet unique.

The Elysium Within

In the depths, a garden blooms,
Nurtured by love, dispelling glooms,
Peace arises, casting fumes,
Elysium, where the spirit looms.

With each breath, a sacred hymn,
Melodies that softly brim,
Reaching heights, though shadows dim,
In the heart, the light grows grim.

The beauty lies in every thought,
In the battles bravely fought,
Through the trials, wisdom's sought,
In the silence, joy is caught.

Here within, the soul's abode,
Walking softly on this road,
Love and grace, the greater code,
In the heart, true peace bestowed.

Elysium knows no bounds,
In the whispers, grace surrounds,
Where the spirit freely grounds,
In unity, the truth resounds.

A Tapestry of Sacred Connections

In whispers soft, the prayers ascend,
A tapestry, where hearts blend.
Each thread a story, woven tight,
In faith's embrace, we find our light.

With every step upon this path,
We feel the presence—endless wrath.
Yet gentleness wraps the fierce embrace,
In stillness, we find our sacred grace.

The mountains bow, the rivers sing,
To ancient truths, our spirits cling.
Beneath the stars, the night reveals,
A unity that time conceals.

In fellowship, we gather near,
A sanctuary, free from fear.
The bonds of love, so deep and wide,
In every heart, our souls abide.

So join the chorus, let it rise,
With every echo, through the skies.
In this grand weave, we do not stand,
But walk together, hand in hand.

Where Grace and Heart Intertwine

In the stillness, grace unfolds,
Stories of love, eternally told.
Hearts reach out, and hands embrace,
In sacred rhythm, we find our place.

Echoes of kindness, softly shared,
In gentle whispers, we are stirred.
Together we journey, side by side,
As hope ignites, our fears subside.

In every struggle, light is drawn,
Through darkest night, we find the dawn.
With every tear, a seed is sown,
In tender grace, we find our home.

A melody of faith and trust,
In every heartbeat, love is a must.
Through valleys low, and mountains high,
The spirit soars, it cannot die.

Let hearts entwine in perfect rhyme,
In every moment, a taste of time.
For in this dance, we are divine,
Where grace and heart forever shine.

The Solace in Reverent Silence

In quiet moments, still and pure,
The soul finds solace, deep and sure.
Beneath the weight of worldly sound,
In silence, sacred truths abound.

The breath of life, a gentle sigh,
In reverence, we look to the sky.
Each heartbeat whispers ancient lore,
In stillness, we unlock the door.

Through quietude, the spirit speaks,
A tender voice, in silence seeks.
The peace that passes understanding,
In every breath, our hearts are landing.

We gaze within, the light reveals,
The mysteries that silence heals.
In shadows cast by doubts and fears,
We find the strength to face our years.

So cherish silence, hold it near,
In every stillness, God is here.
With open hearts, we find our way,
In reverent silence, we shall stay.

Promises Written in Celestial Light

Under the stars, our dreams take flight,
Promises whispered, clear and bright.
In celestial dance, we trust the night,
With faith as our guide, we seek the light.

Each shining star a hope bestowed,
In cosmic wonders, our spirits rode.
The universe speaks in gentle tones,
In every heartbeat, we're never alone.

In depths of darkness, we find the spark,
Illuminating paths through the dark.
With every shadow, a truth ignites,
In silent prayers, we claim our rights.

Promises woven in fate's embrace,
In every journey, we find our place.
With hands uplifted, we call the night,
As stars align, guiding our sight.

So look above, where dreams collide,
With every heartbeat, love our guide.
In cosmic light, together we stand,
With promises written, hand in hand.

Celestial Mapping of the Soul

In the realms where starlight weaves,
The spirit finds its guiding stars,
Each twinkle whispers ancient truths,
Mapping pathways of the soul.

Through cosmic charts of love and grace,
The heart expands, embraces light,
In every shadow, hope ignites,
Awakening the dormant dreams.

Galaxies of thought collide,
In the silence, wisdom speaks,
A dance with fate, the sacred vows,
Embracing all that's yet to come.

Charting dreams in skies untamed,
With every beat, the pulse of time,
The universe inside us hums,
Drawing depth from storms endured.

So let us fly on wings of faith,
To realms where truth and love combine,
Mapping stars that shine within,
Guiding souls back home to light.

A Rite of Passage to Acceptance

In the quiet dawn of understanding,
We shed the fears that dim our light,
With open arms, we greet the truth,
Embracing all that we have been.

Each wound a lesson, softly spoken,
Beneath the scars, a heart beats strong,
In vulnerability, we find our strength,
A rite of passage to belong.

The mirrors that reflect our journey,
Show flaws and beauty intertwined,
In every glance, a tale unfolding,
Acceptance blooms within the heart.

Let go the chains of doubt and sorrow,
And feel the freedom of release,
In the gentle breath of acceptance,
We find our spirits' sweet reprise.

As we walk the path of self-discovery,
Each step a dance with grace anew,
In every moment, let love guide,
A sacred gift, forever true.

The Language of the Heart's Echo

In whispers soft as evening's breath,
The heart speaks truths beyond mere words,
A symphony of silent echoes,
Resonating through the soul's vastness.

Every tear is a note of longing,
Every smile, a song of grace,
In laughter rich as golden mornings,
The heart conveys its purest face.

Through trials faced, the heart speaks loud,
In valleys deep, and mountains high,
Though silent, it conveys our essence,
An unbroken line to the divine.

The sacred rhythm beats inside us,
A connection to the great unknown,
In every pulse, the love of ages,
Echoing the language of the heart.

So listen closely to the music,
Let your spirit dance to its call,
For in the echoes of our being,
Is the truth that unites us all.

Embracing the Quietude of Being

In stillness, grace begins to flourish,
The noise of life begins to fade,
In moments pure, the soul can wander,
Embracing peace in silent waves.

The heart finds solace in the quiet,
Where whispers of the divine unfold,
In every pause, a gentle knowing,
A deep connection to the whole.

Through seasons marked by chaos' hand,
We find the strength to just be still,
In the sanctuary of our being,
We meet the essence of our will.

Let the world rush on around us,
In silence, we can breathe and dream,
In the depths of this calm embrace,
Our spirits rise, united, free.

So treasure every fleeting moment,
In the quietude, let love dwell,
For in this stillness, we discover,
The sacred truth we long to tell.

The Heart's Sacred Manifesto

In silence I seek the light,
Whispers of grace take flight.
With each beat, my soul ascends,
Love's echo, my heart defends.

In shadows, I find the truth,
Guide me back to my youth.
With humbleness, I surrender,
To the Spirit, my defender.

In prayer, I weave my dreams,
Flowing like sacred streams.
Through trials, my faith grows strong,
In harmony, I belong.

With every breath, I proclaim,
To the world, His holy name.
In the stillness, I will praise,
For His mercy lights my days.

In unity, I stand with grace,
With compassion, we embrace.
Together, we walk this path,
In love's light, we feel no wrath.

Harmonies of the Inner Sanctuary

In the quiet, I hear the call,
A symphony beyond the wall.
Each note a prayer, pure and bright,
Guiding me through the night.

Within the heart's sacred shell,
Echoes of wisdom dwell.
Harmony flows like a stream,
In this space, I dare to dream.

Colors of faith and love blend,
A tapestry that will not end.
In meditation, I find my peace,
From worldly troubles, I release.

Together, we gather and sing,
For joy and hope are offering.
In every voice, a story found,
Creating a circle, profound.

In this haven, we shall grow,
With open hearts, we let love flow.
The sanctuary of the soul, so wide,
In its embrace, we shall abide.

Pilgrimage to the Center of Being

On a path of sacred stone,
Inward journeys I have known.
With faith as my steadfast chart,
I search for the center of my heart.

Mountains high and valleys deep,
In divine presence, I will leap.
With every step, my spirit learns,
In life's wisdom, my heart yearns.

Through trials, my strength will rise,
Guided by the stars and skies.
Each heartbeat a sacred drum,
Calling forth the love to come.

As I wander, the light reveals,
Secrets that my soul conceals.
In the stillness, I find my grace,
A journey home through time and space.

With every footprint laid in prayer,
I seek the truth that leads me there.
To the center where love is king,
In communion, my heart will sing.

The Celestial Dance of the Heart

Stars above in wondrous array,
Guide my heart in the ballet.
With arms wide, I embrace the night,
In the dark, I find the light.

Each rhythm of life a divine beat,
A dance of joy, serene and sweet.
With every twirl, love draws near,
A cosmic bond that knows no fear.

In the silence, the music flows,
Infinite wisdom gently grows.
With grace, I join the sacred rhyme,
In this dance, transcending time.

Together we rise, souls entwined,
In harmony, with hearts aligned.
In the melody of divine grace,
We lose ourselves in love's embrace.

Let the universe spin and sway,
As we dance the night away.
In every heartbeat, a prayer sung,
In life's symphony, we are one.

Pathways to the Eternal Flame

In the quiet dusk, souls tread,
With faith as their guiding thread.
Each footstep leads where love ignites,
In the shadows of sacred nights.

Hearts unite beneath the stars,
Whispering dreams of who we are.
Through trials faced, we rise in grace,
Finding light in every place.

Rivers of mercy flow with ease,
Carrying prayers upon the breeze.
Winds of change come soft and mild,
An embrace given, the heart of a child.

As dawn breaks with golden hue,
Our spirits soar, fresh and new.
In the glow of a burning light,
We walk together, pure delight.

To the flame that cannot wane,
We gather strength through joy and pain.
In each heartbeat, a sacred song,
Together, we learn where we belong.

Gathering the Fragments of Joy

In the garden of laughter blooms,
Filling hearts, dispelling glooms.
Fragments of joy, scattered wide,
In each moment, the love inside.

The morning sun begins to shine,
Kisses of warmth, gentle and fine.
Every smile a sacred gift,
In unity, our spirits lift.

Eager hands reach for the sky,
Each blessing found, a soulful sigh.
Together we weave the threads of grace,
In every heart, a cherished place.

Through trials deep, our spirits mend,
Collecting the pieces, our hearts transcend.
We dance in circles, a joyous sphere,
Gathering love, erasing fear.

In the twilight glow, we stand as one,
Greeting the night when the day is done.
With every star, our dreams align,
Fragments of joy, forever divine.

The Pilgrim's Embrace

With weary feet, the pilgrim walks,
Through winding paths and sacred talks.
Each step a prayer, each breath a sigh,
In the stillness, the soul learns to fly.

Mountains rise to touch the sky,
Whispers of faith from deep inside.
In every valley kissed by light,
The spirit dances, hearts take flight.

Through stormy nights and sunny days,
The journey unfolds in countless ways.
Embracing hardships, we find our peace,
In pilgrimage, our doubts release.

With open arms, the world we greet,
Finding solace in every beat.
Together we share the sacred space,
In every gaze, the pilgrim's grace.

Our hearts entwined, we forge ahead,
By love's pure light, we are led.
Through every challenge, we remain,
In the embrace of the spirit's reign.

Seeking Sanctuary in Stillness

In the hush of dawn, silence sings,
Cradled in peace, the spirit clings.
In stillness found, the heart's refrain,
Seeking solace, we break the chain.

Moments of quiet, breaths so deep,
In sacred stillness, the soul will seep.
Waves of calm wash over strife,
Finding refuge in the dance of life.

Beneath the trees, where shadows play,
We gather wisdom at the end of day.
Each whisper soft, a gentle guide,
In this sanctuary, we abide.

The stars reveal their hidden grace,
In their light, we find our place.
With open hearts, we greet the night,
Seeking sanctuary, hearts take flight.

In meditation's warm embrace,
We discover truth, divine and trace.
In stillness, life's essence flows,
Embraced by love, our spirit knows.

The Soul's Resonant Journey

In the stillness of the night,
Whispers of faith take flight.
Eternal paths, so intertwined,
In the heart, the truth you find.

With every step, a chance to rise,
Beneath the vast, unending skies.
The spirit sails on winds of grace,
Finding solace in sacred space.

In shadows deep, a light will gleam,
Guiding souls toward the dream.
Each note of love, a sacred song,
In unity, we all belong.

Through valleys low and mountains high,
A journey led by the divine.
With open hearts and open hands,
We walk together, as the heart commands.

So let the soul's deep echo sound,
In the love that's all around.
For in this journey, we shall see,
The boundless grace that sets us free.

In the Footsteps of the Divine Path

Upon the road where truth unfolds,
In whispers soft, the story told.
With every stride, the spirit dances,
In faith's embrace, our soul advances.

The sun may rise, the shadows fall,
Yet in the heart, there echoes call.
To follow where the light does lead,
In humble prayer, we plant the seed.

With open eyes, we see the signs,
In every heart, the love entwines.
Beneath the firmament so wide,
We seek the source, the sacred guide.

Each step a prayer, each breath a vow,
Together in the here and now.
In gratitude, we lift our song,
As we journey, we grow strong.

In steadfast hope, we find our way,
In every night that turns to day.
The path is drawn, the stars align,
In the footsteps of the divine.

The Heart's Litany of Longing

In silence deep, the heart does yearn,
For love's embrace, a sacred turn.
With every beat, the pulse of grace,
In longing, we find our place.

The spirit calls in whispered tones,
In every prayer, the heart atones.
A yearning soul, a light untamed,
In love's own name, we are reclaimed.

As shadows fade, and dawn breaks clear,
In every tear, the joy we steer.
For in the longing, faith takes flight,
Transforming darkness into light.

With open arms, we seek the real,
In every touch, divine we feel.
The heart's litany, a sacred chant,
In anguish, hope begins to plant.

Through valleys low, to mountains peak,
In longing's journey, truth we seek.
The heart's desire, a flame so bright,
Guided by love, we chase the light.

Celestial Bridges to Inner Harmony

In quietude, the spirit soars,
As heaven's whispers gently pours.
Each thought a bridge, each prayer a stream,
In inner peace, we dare to dream.

The stars above, a guiding creed,
Reminding us of love's pure need.
In unity, our voices blend,
To seek the truths that never end.

Through trials faced and lessons learned,
In every heart, a flame is burned.
With open minds, we seek the whole,
Connecting each with every soul.

In laughter shared and tears released,
We find the grace that gives us peace.
Celestial paths, we walk as one,
In harmony, our fears undone.

From depths of silence, beauty springs,
In grateful hearts, the spirit sings.
Together, we rise, lifted high,
On celestial bridges, we touch the sky.

Love Letters from the Infinite

In twilight whispers, love divine,
Hearts entwined with threads of light,
Each word, a blessing from above,
Echoing softly through the night.

Across the heavens, stars align,
Guiding souls with gentle grace,
Each letter penned, a sacred sign,
Unfurling love in every space.

In silence echoes, truths unfold,
A tapestry of faith and peace,
Each heartbeat tells the tales of old,
Where love and hope shall never cease.

Embraced by spirits, strong and bold,
Infinite love's tender call,
In shadows cast, bright stories told,
In every rise, we'll never fall.

And so, dear heart, keep near this flame,
In every journey, light your way,
For all the letters bear His name,
In love and faith, we forever stay.

Stones of Wisdom on the Path

Upon the earth, the stones are laid,
Each one a lesson from the past,
With every step, our souls are made,
In trials faced, our spirits cast.

The winds of change, they gently blow,
Whispering secrets in the night,
With every stone, our hearts will grow,
In wisdom's warmth, we find the light.

The journey's long, but we are strong,
With faith as our unwavering guide,
From stony trials, we learn the song,
Of unity and love, our pride.

Each grain of sand, a world refined,
Beneath our feet, the truth resides,
In every corner, hope we find,
Along this path our spirit glides.

Together we tread, through night and day,
With stones of wisdom, hearts ignited,
In every step, we choose to stay,
In peace and love, forever united.

A Song of the Soul's Redemption

Awake, my soul, arise and sing,
The dawn whispers of grace anew,
In every heart, redemption's spring,
A melody of love so true.

Through valleys deep, and mountains high,
The journey's song resounds with peace,
In every tear, a reason why,
In every trial, our hearts release.

O sweet refrain, breathe life to dreams,
In shadows cast, let hope ignite,
For every soul is sewn with seams,
Of love's embrace, in darkest night.

In the rivers of grace, we flow,
Each note a prayer, a gentle sigh,
Through every storm, together grow,
Bound by faith, our spirits fly.

When all is sung, united we stand,
In harmony, our voices blend,
For in this song, we take His hand,
A dance of love that knows no end.

The Breath of the Beloved

In quiet moments, breathe the love,
In every sigh, the sacred speaks,
The breath of life, a gift above,
With every heartbeat, the spirit seeks.

Through valleys wide and mountains tall,
In every whisper, feel Him near,
For in the silence, we can call,
The essence of the One we hold dear.

With every dawn, a promise glows,
The breath of the Beloved remains,
In gentle winds, His grace bestows,
In every joy, in every pain.

In moments still, feel love abide,
With open hearts, we find our way,
In every breath, our souls collide,
Creating light to guide the day.

So let each breath, a prayer arise,
In harmony with life's sweet song,
In love, we find our true allies,
With every breath, our hearts belong.

Visions of a Heart Reclaimed

In shadows deep, a light arose,
A whisper soft, the heart it chose.
From ashes born, a flame ignites,
In love's embrace, the soul delights.

With every step, the path unfolds,
A tapestry of stories told.
In faith we walk, hand in hand,
Together we shall make our stand.

The chains unbind, the spirit soars,
A joyful hymn from open doors.
In grace we find our truest way,
A radiant dawn to bless the day.

Through trials faced and battles won,
A sacred bond with the Holy One.
In every tear, a lesson learned,
A heart reclaimed, a passion burned.

Eternal love, our guiding star,
In every moment, near or far.
With open hearts, we seek to share,
The visions bright of love and care.

Psalms of the Wanderer

From mountain high to valley low,
The wanderer walks where spirits flow.
In silence deep, a voice will call,
To lift the heart through fears that fall.

With weary feet on winding trails,
The heart shall sing where hope prevails.
In every shadow, light breaks through,
In faithful hearts, the promise true.

For every step upon this land,
The touch of grace, a guiding hand.
In nature's hymn, the soul finds peace,
A melody that shall not cease.

Through storms we face, the sky so wide,
The heart can soar on love's great tide.
With every loss, a lesson gained,
In every prayer, our faith remained.

The wanderer's path, though filled with doubt,
In every drop, the love flows out.
With open heart, we find our way,
In every night, there shines a day.

The Dance of Spirit and Truth

In every heartbeat, a rhythm flows,
A sacred dance that gently grows.
With open eyes, the spirit moves,
In every truth that love approves.

Around the fire, the watchers sing,
A melody of the heart's offering.
In sacred space, we find our grace,
Unity in this holy place.

With every tear, a promise shared,
In every smile, the love declared.
The dance of life, both wild and free,
In harmony, we long to be.

In whispers low, the spirit calls,
In every chamber, where love enthralls.
We twirl in faith, and love's embrace,
In every moment, find our place.

With open hearts, we yield our fears,
In every laugh, the joy appears.
Together in this dance we find,
The spirit's truth, forever kind.

Lost and Found in Reverence

In quiet corners, hearts entwined,
A sacred space where love is blind.
In loss, we grieve, but soon we see,
In reverence, we seek to be free.

With every tear, a seed is sown,
In empty spaces, love has grown.
Through shadows cast, the light does shine,
In every heart, a sacred sign.

The journeys long, yet wisdom flows,
From every trial, the spirit knows.
In trust we rise, in hope we stand,
With open hearts, we join the band.

As petals fall, and seasons change,
The cycle turns, yet love feels strange.
In sacred time, we learn to see,
In reverence, we find the key.

For every soul that's felt alone,
In every heart, a flame has grown.
In loss we find, and love we've crowned,
In reverence, we are lost and found.

Illuminating the Shadows of My Being

In quiet corners, shadows creep,
They whisper secrets, buried deep.
Yet in the dark, a light shines clear,
Guiding my heart, dispelling fear.

With gentle hands, the Spirit molds,
A tapestry of grace unfolds.
Each thread a prayer, a sacred sound,
In solitude, true strength is found.

The dawn awakens, hope's embrace,
Illumined paths of holy space.
Every burden, lifted high,
Together with faith, we touch the sky.

In shadows deep, love's whisper calls,
Through endless night, true light still falls.
Embracing truths, both lost and found,
In every soul, the love is bound.

Journey onward, heart in hand,
With faith as compass, we will stand.
Illuminating paths unseen,
The sacred dance, a holy dream.

The Flame that Unites and Heals

Within the heart, a flame does burn,
A beacon bright, for all we yearn.
In every breath, a prayer ignites,
Uniting souls on sacred nights.

Through trials faced, we gather near,
Each whispered word, a song sincere.
The fire of love dispels the cold,
In its warm glow, the truth unfolds.

With hands embraced, we rise as one,
A harmonious tune, life's song begun.
As spirits dance, the darkness flees,
In unity, we find our peace.

Each flicker bright, a sign of grace,
Illuminating every place.
A healing balm for weary hearts,
The Flame that heals, from which love starts.

We share the light, in joy we stand,
Together stronger, hand in hand.
As flames unite, our spirits soar,
In love's embrace, forever more.

Chasing the Divine Pulse of Life

In nature's breath, I hear the call,
The pulse of life, in rise and fall.
Each heartbeat echoes, soft and true,
Chasing the light, where grace breaks through.

With open eyes, the world unfolds,
The beauty found in stories told.
In laughter shared and tears embraced,
The dance of life, divinely laced.

The currents flow, in endless streams,
In sacred moments, we weave dreams.
Each step we take, a prayer in flight,
Chasing the star, igniting the night.

In every soul, the Echo rings,
A melody of holy things.
With hearts aligned, we seek the grace,
The pulse of life, a warm embrace.

Awakened by the love we share,
The journey's gift, beyond compare.
In each heartbeat, the truth is known,
Chasing the divine, we are never alone.

The Mosaic of Blissful Grace

In fragments scattered, beauty lies,
Each piece a glimpse of heaven's skies.
Together they form a sacred whole,
A mosaic bright, a spirit's soul.

Through trials faced and dreams pursued,
In every heart, the spark imbued.
We shape our lives with colors bold,
In unity, the heart unfolds.

With gentle hands, we craft and mend,
In love's embrace, all wounds can bend.
Each shard a story, unique, divine,
In this great art, our souls entwine.

The patterns shift with every breath,
In life's mosaic, we conquer death.
With faith as glue, our spirits rise,
A harmony of truths and ties.

In joyful chaos, grace appears,
A song of life, dissolving fears.
Each moment shared, a sacred trace,
Creating the mosaic of blissful grace.

Journeying Through Sacred Echoes

In the quiet of the night, I tread,
Whispers of the ancients are widespread.
Stars above, they guide my way,
Their light reveals the path to stay.

Each step a prayer, each breath a song,
In the arms of faith, where I belong.
Carried by the wind, my spirit soars,
Through echoes of love, my heart implores.

In shadows cast by moonlit beams,
I find solace in the sacred dreams.
These echoes speak of grace and peace,
In their embrace, all sorrows cease.

With every heartbeat, a sacred drum,
Reminds me of the love to come.
Journeying where the faithful dwell,
In sacred whispers, all is well.

The Stillness in My Heart's Chapel

Within my heart, a chapel stands,
Built by faith and gentle hands.
In stillness, secrets softly bloom,
A sacred light dispels the gloom.

Here silence sings of grace divine,
In each quiet moment, I align.
The whispers of the soul resound,
In this hallowed space, I am crowned.

Still waters mirror the sky's embrace,
Reflecting love, a holy grace.
In prayer, I seek the truth so pure,
In stillness, my spirit finds allure.

The walls adorned with hope's great light,
Guide me through the darkest night.
In my heart's chapel, I am free,
In sacred stillness, I find me.

An Offering to the Infinite

With open hands, I give my all,
An offering to the One who calls.
In humble pots of clay, I stand,
To show my love across the land.

Each tear a token, each smile a prayer,
A heart laid bare, in reverent care.
The infinite embraces my small gift,
In this act of love, my spirits lift.

Oceans of grace pour from above,
As I surrender to endless love.
In sacred moments, I feel His sigh,
An invitation to soar and fly.

With gratitude, I walk this path,
In the shadows, I find the light's wrath.
Each offering embraced, a sacred tie,
Linked to eternity, I learn to fly.

Where Love Meets the Divine

In the embrace of twilight's grace,
I find the love that time cannot erase.
Where shadows dance and spirits glide,
In this sacred space, we abide.

Each heartbeat whispers a timeless tune,
In love's pure light, the soul attunes.
Where the divine touches human skin,
A cosmic dance where we begin.

Under the stars, our prayers entwine,
In the depth of night, love and divinity shine.
Together we weave a tapestry bright,
Where we find comfort in love's pure light.

As rivers meet the endless sea,
I find the divine within me.
In every moment, a holy spark,
Where love illuminates the dark.

Whispers from the Divine Within

In silence I await Your call,
A gentle breeze, a feathered fall.
Your whispers guide my longing heart,
To seek the light, to play my part.

Each thought a prayer, each breath a song,
In every moment, I belong.
The hush of night, the break of day,
Your presence dawns, showing the way.

A starry sky, a sacred space,
Reflections of Your boundless grace.
In shadows cast, I feel the light,
Illuminating darkest night.

With every step, I walk in trust,
Feelings raw, yet born of love.
The path is steep, yet I am strong,
For in Your love, I find my song.

So here I stand, a humble heart,
Longing to learn, longing to start.
Your whispers echo deep within,
A sacred journey, where love begins.

The Pilgrimage to Inner Serenity

With weary feet, the path unfolds,
In search of peace, as truth enfolds.
Each step a prayer upon the ground,
The soul's deep call, in silence found.

The mountains high, the valleys wide,
A journey made with faith as guide.
Through trials faced and shadows cast,
I find the strength to hold steadfast.

In every breath, a moment's grace,
For in the stillness, I find place.
The whispers of an ancient creed,
Flow through my spirit, plant the seed.

The rivers flow, they sing my way,
As nature's voice begins to play.
In every leaf, a testament,
Of love and light, divinely sent.

And as I pause, my heart ignites,
In sacred spaces, pure delights.
The pilgrimage, a journey true,
To find the joy that's born anew.

A Love Written in Celestial Ink

In heavens high, our story's penned,
A love so deep, that knows no end.
In every star, Your whispers shine,
A sacred bond, forever mine.

Through trials faced, we stand as one,
A tapestry of moon and sun.
Each moment shared, a treasured page,
In divine love, we find our stage.

With every touch, the universe sways,
A dance of souls in cosmic ways.
In tender grace, our spirits soar,
For love transcends, forevermore.

The ink may fade, but hearts will glow,
In every heartbeat, love will grow.
Each word a promise, sworn and true,
A love eternal, just me and you.

With every dawn, a chance to start,
The stories etched within my heart.
So here we stand, together linked,
In every breath, celestial ink.

Echoes of the Heart's True Calling

In every whisper of the breeze,
The heart awakes, its song to please.
A calling strong, a deep refrain,
To seek the truth beyond the pain.

With open arms to skies above,
I feel the pulse of endless love.
In silence found, the echoes ring,
Of deeper truths that living bring.

Each moment here is blessed with grace,
In gentle sighs, I find Your face.
The heart unfurls, like petals wide,
In every beat, You are my guide.

Through valleys low and mountains high,
The calling comes with each soft sigh.
For in my soul, You light the way,
A promise pure, that will not sway.

As shadows dance in fading light,
The echoes speak of morning bright.
In every tear, a joy concealed,
The heart's true calling is revealed.

The Light Within the Shadows

In stillness lies a sacred spark,
A whisper between the dark.
Hope glimmers in the night,
Guiding souls towards the light.

Every shadow holds a grace,
In trials, we see His face.
With faith, the heart will grow,
In darkness, love will flow.

The path may twist and turn,
Yet within, the embers burn.
With prayer, we seek and find,
The light that frees the mind.

Beneath the weight of worldly woes,
A deeper truth gently glows.
In quiet corners, wisdom waits,
To show us how hope creates.

So let us walk without despair,
In shadows, we find His care.
For even in the night's embrace,
We carry forth the light of grace.

Chasing the Celestial Flame

Upon the hills, the embers soar,
A glowing touch of evermore.
The flame leads hearts to seek,
In silence, it begins to speak.

Through valleys deep and skies of blue,
The fire calls, it beckons true.
With every step, the spirit bends,
In love, each journey transcends.

Beyond the stars, our spirits chase,
An endless quest for grace.
With faith as our guiding star,
We journey forth, no distance far.

To chase the flame is to believe,
In all the gifts that life can weave.
For every heart that dares to dream,
Shall find the light within its beam.

So hold the flame and let it grow,
In every heart, let kindness flow.
Chasing fire from above,
We dance beneath the stars of love.

Beneath the Veil of Seraphs

Beneath the wings of holy light,
Cherubs sing through endless night.
In sacred space, we hear their songs,
Where every heart and spirit belongs.

In whispers soft, they guide us near,
In every joy, in every tear.
With every breath, we feel their grace,
Embracing all in love's embrace.

The beauty found in heaven's glow,
In light and shadow, we shall grow.
With seraphs near, we learn to see,
The boundless love that sets us free.

Their laughter dances in the air,
An echo sweet, beyond compare.
Through trials faced, we find our way,
In love's surrender, night turns to day.

So let our hearts in faith unite,
Beneath the veil, we share the light.
For in this journey, we do find,
The love of heaven intertwined.

The Quest for Sacred Wholeness

In the tapestry of time we weave,
A quest for wholeness we believe.
With every thread, a sacred art,
A journey born within the heart.

In moments quiet, we reflect,
On paths of faith we still respect.
For every tear and every smile,
Brings us closer, mile by mile.

The quest unfolds in grace's name,
In love's embrace, we fan the flame.
Through trials faced, we find our strength,
In sacred circles, love's great length.

So gather near and hear the call,
In unity, we rise, not fall.
For in our hearts, the truth does dwell,
A story shared, a sacred tell.

Together, let our spirits soar,
In quest for wholeness, we implore.
With open hearts and hands entwined,
In love, our sacred truth we find.

Sacred Reflections in Still Waters

In still waters, truth does glide,
Mirrors of faith, where spirits reside.
Whispers of grace in tranquil night,
Guiding the heart towards the light.

Ripples of prayer, softly awake,
In the depths, the soul shall take.
Each drop a promise, every wave,
A dance of hope, the heart must save.

Beneath the surface, a world so vast,
In silent reflections, shadows cast.
Each thought a prayer, each sigh a plea,
In sacred waters, I find Thee.

With humble heart, I kneel and bow,
To the stillness that breathes right now.
In dreams of patience and kindness shown,
The divine voice calls me home.

Let me linger by this holy shore,
In contemplation, I crave You more.
For in moments of silence, I see,
The heart's desire, my soul set free.

The Altar of Yearning and Belonging

Upon this altar, dreams ignite,
Yearnings deep as day turns night.
In every tear, a whisper shared,
In every prayer, a heart laid bare.

Candles flicker, hopes alight,
Ghosts of longing, gathering tight.
Each sacrifice, a story told,
Of faith unbroken, hearts so bold.

In the silence, we find our place,
The warmth of love, the touch of grace.
In unity, our spirits blend,
A sacred bond that will not end.

Let every flame dance in the air,
Reminders of our solemn care.
For in this harmony, we belong,
Together, we create our song.

To the altar of hopes, we come drawn,
In our sharing, we find the dawn.
With open hearts, we belove and lift,
The sacred bond is our greatest gift.

In Pursuit of the Divine Echo

In quiet woods, I hear the call,
A soft refrain, the echo of all.
Each leaf a story, every breeze,
Carries whispers that put me at ease.

Footsteps light on sacred ground,
In pursuit of the lost sound.
Searching fervently, heart in flight,
For the divine in the veil of night.

Reflections shimmer on water's face,
Nature's canvas, an embrace of grace.
In every moment, I seek and yearn,
For the echo of love in return.

Through valleys deep and mountains high,
I wander forth, unafraid to cry.
In redemption's song, my spirit soars,
Through valleys of doubt, towards heaven's doors.

In pursuit of truth, with heart sincere,
I chase the light, I conquer fear.
For in every echo, I find my way,
Drawn ever closer to the sacred sway.

The Scroll of My Affection

Upon this scroll, my love I write,
In verses soft, like stars at night.
Each word a gesture of my heart,
In every line, a work of art.

Ink flows freely, emotions bare,
A testament of love and care.
In each loop and curve, a promise true,
A declaration, forever due.

For in the margins, memories weave,
Stories of people, in whom I believe.
Through trials faced and sorrows shared,
My soul's reflection, tenderly bared.

The parchment cradles hopes and dreams,
Each tale of joy, softly gleams.
In peace and chaos, love shall reign,
A scroll of affection, devoid of pain.

As I inscribe the journey's course,
With every stroke, I feel the force.
A sacred love that will not fade,
For within this scroll, my heart's displayed.

In twilight's glow, the ink shall dry,
But in my heart, love will not die.
For every letter penned in grace,
Is an echo of the sacred space.

A Heart Awakened by Sacred Dreams

In quiet whispers of the night,
The soul unfolds, bathed in light.
Awakening to the sacred call,
With faith, we rise, we will not fall.

A journey sparked by divine grace,
Every heartbeat finds its place.
With prayer, the spirit takes flight,
In shadows found, we seek the bright.

Each vision shared, a glimpse of truth,
In innocence lies eternal youth.
A tapestry woven with care,
In dreams, we find the love we share.

Together we walk on sacred ground,
In every sound, His love is found.
With open hearts and hopeful sighs,
We dance beneath the endless skies.

For in this realm of blissful peace,
Where all our sorrows find release,
A heart awakened, forever gleams,
In unity, we live our dreams.

The Luminescence of Inner Beacons

In every soul, a light does glow,
A spark ignited, with love to show.
Through trials faced and storms we brave,
The inner beacon guides, we save.

From darkness deep, our truths emerge,
With every breath, the spirits surge.
A path illuminated, bright and clear,
In whispers soft, we choose to hear.

With courage drawn from silent wells,
In every story, the spirit dwells.
The luminescence of hope unfolds,
In gentle arms, our hearts consoled.

As stars align in skies above,
We find our place, we find our love.
With hands embraced, we walk the way,
In unity, we greet the day.

Embrace the light that shines within,
For in that glow, our souls begin.
With every step, our spirits soar,
In sacred grace, forevermore.

The Divine Artistry of Love

In strokes of grace the heart is drawn,
A masterpiece at each new dawn.
With tender hands, the soul creates,
A world alive, where love awaits.

Through every challenge, hope will bloom,
In shadows cast, love finds the room.
A canvas painted, rich and bright,
In every hue, the spirit's light.

With whispered prayers, our voices blend,
Upon this path, together we mend.
The divine artistry unfolds,
In stories shared, the heart beholds.

As seasons change, our hearts entwine,
In sacred rhythm, His love aligns.
With every pulse, our spirits dance,
In love's embrace, we find our chance.

For in this journey, we discover,
The greatest masterpiece: each other.
With open hearts, and spirits free,
Together, we create our destiny.

Embracing the Spirit's Serenade

In the stillness, a melody calls,
The spirit sings, where silence falls.
With every note, a whisper sweet,
In harmony, our souls shall meet.

The echoes rise through gentle air,
Inviting all to join in prayer.
With open hearts, our voices soar,
Embracing love forevermore.

As nature hums its sacred song,
In every breath, we all belong.
The spirit dances in the breeze,
With every sway, our worries ease.

Through twilight hues, the day concludes,
In quiet joy, our love imbues.
With arms outstretched, we seek the light,
Embracing all that feels so right.

For in this serenade divine,
We find our strength, our faith aligns.
In every heart, the song remains,
Embracing love through joy and pains.

Harmony in the Temple of Being

In sacred halls where whispers dwell,
Each breath, a prayer, a story to tell.
The heartbeats sync with nature's tune,
As souls ascend beneath the moon.

Unity we seek, a bond divine,
In tranquil moments, our spirits align.
With every thought, the light we share,
A tapestry woven with love and care.

The gentle breeze carries our dreams,
Through corridors where silence beams.
In this temple, we find our peace,
A realm where all doubt and fear cease.

Voices blend in harmonious cheer,
Each note a promise, drawing us near.
With open hearts, we embrace the grace,
In the temple of being, we find our place.

Eternal echoes in shadows play,
Guiding us through the night and day.
In this harmony, we're not alone,
Together we flourish, forever known.

The Light that Guides My Inner Quest

In the stillness of dawn's first light,
A whisper stirs, dispelling the night.
This gentle glow, my guiding star,
Illuminates paths both near and far.

With each step taken upon life's road,
I carry faith, a sacred load.
The light within, a flame so true,
Awakens courage to see anew.

In moments of doubt, I pause and pray,
Trusting the light will show the way.
A beacon bright in the darkest seas,
It fills my heart with tranquil ease.

As I journey through valleys deep,
The light remains, a watchful keep.
It weaves through shadows, dispelling fears,
A sacred promise through the years.

In the fullness of night, stars ignite,
Mirrors of hope, reflecting the light.
I tread with joy, my spirit blessed,
Forever guided on this inner quest.

Beneath the Veil of Stars

In quiet nights under velvet skies,
I find my solace where wonder lies.
Stars like whispers, secrets they share,
Painting dreams with celestial flair.

Beneath their gaze, the world feels small,
Yet in their glow, I feel it all.
Each shimmering light, a story untold,
Of love and loss, both tender and bold.

I reach for wisdom in the stillness,
Finding truth within the thrill of this.
Galaxies swirl in sacred dance,
Inviting my spirit to take a chance.

In the silence, I hear their song,
A melody of the universe, strong.
Guiding me home through the darkest night,
To the deepest corner of inner light.

Beneath the veil, I breathe the grace,
Each star a mirror of the divine embrace.
Connected to all, I rise and fall,
In the cosmic symphony, I hear the call.

The Oracle of My Silent Yearnings

In shadows deep, a oracle waits,
Holding secrets of love and fates.
With whispers soft, it calls my name,
Awakening dreams, igniting the flame.

In the stillness, I find my voice,
Listening closely, I make my choice.
Yearnings rise, like incense in air,
A sacred dance, a silent prayer.

Through time and space, the heart takes flight,
Guiding my soul with radiant light.
The oracle speaks in gentle ways,
Revealing truths in life's winding maze.

Transforming pain into sweet release,
In its embrace, I find my peace.
Mysteries unfold, as I trust and learn,
In the quiet, my spirit will burn.

With open heart, I face the dawn,
The oracle's gift, a love reborn.
In every yearning, I hear the call,
A divine journey, embracing it all.

The Prayer of the Searching Heart

In the stillness, I seek Thy grace,
Whispers of hope in this sacred space.
A longing soul, with arms open wide,
Trusting in You, my eternal guide.

With every tear, a prayer I send,
Yearning for peace, my heart to mend.
Light my path through shadows of night,
Illuminate dreams, lead me to light.

In silence, I find my voice anew,
Strengthened by faith, my spirit true.
A humble heart, I lay at Thy feet,
Searching for solace in love's heartbeat.

Grant me wisdom, show me the way,
In every obstacle, let hope stay.
For in the trials, Thy love does grow,
A prayerful heart in Thy hands shall glow.

So here I stand, open and bare,
A searching heart filled with Thy care.
In this journey, I trust and believe,
With every prayer, Thy grace I receive.

Weaving Dreams into Destiny

In the loom of life, threads intertwine,
Each dream a color, vibrant, divine.
With faith as the needle, I stitch with care,
Weaving my hopes into God's loving prayer.

In moments of doubt, the tension may rise,
Yet in the struggle, the beauty lies.
Through trials faced, I learn to be free,
In the tapestry woven, Your love I see.

The patterns evolve, from sorrow to light,
Every shadow transformed, a guiding insight.
As dreams take flight, anchored in grace,
I find my destiny in Your embrace.

With every heartbeat, my vision expands,
Embracing the journey, I trust in Your hands.
The fabric of life, rich and profound,
In every stitch, Your blessings abound.

So let the threads dance, vibrant and bold,
In the fabric of faith, my story unfolds.
Together we weave, Your dreams and mine,
Creating a destiny, lovingly divine.

The Bridge to Wholeness

Across the chasm, I see Your light,
A bridge of love, strong and bright.
With every step on this sacred way,
I find my heart, where it longs to stay.

In the quiet moments, hear my plea,
A longing for wholeness, come set me free.
With faith as my compass, I walk this path,
Guided by grace through love's gentle wrath.

The waters may rage, yet I will not fall,
For You are my refuge, my all in all.
With each heartbeat, a promise I claim,
In Your embrace, I find my true name.

As I cross this bridge, burdens set down,
Each step I take, in love I am found.
Your light shines bright, dispelling the dark,
In the journey of faith, I re-discover spark.

Now at journey's end, in wholeness I stand,
Connected by love, hand in hand.
Your presence enfolds me, serene and grand,
In the bridge of Your heart, forever I land.

Songs from Forgotten Sanctuaries

In the echoes of time, sweet melodies rise,
Songs of the faithful, beneath ancient skies.
Resounding in chambers where whispers reside,
Forgotten sanctuaries where hearts confide.

Each note a prayer, soft as the dawn,
Reviving the spirit, awakening grace drawn.
In the silence, a harmony flows,
Unveiling the truths that our spirit knows.

From shadows of doubt, to the light of belief,
These sacred songs offer solace and relief.
In every refrain, a promise to renew,
The forgotten places awaken to You.

Let the hymns of yesterday call us to rise,
Guiding our hearts to the heavens' prize.
For in these sanctuaries, our souls find peace,
In songs of the past, sweet love will increase.

So gather these melodies, let them take flight,
In forgotten sanctuaries, we find the light.
Together in spirit, united in song,
In the heart's pure sanctuary, we all belong.

Surrender to the Sacred Flow

In stillness, find the gentle stream,
Let the heart weave with the divine beam.
With each breath, give in to grace,
Trust the path, the sacred space.

Wash away the fears that bind,
Feel the presence, pure and kind.
As waves of love lift the soul,
Surrender deep, be made whole.

In silence, wisdom softly calls,
Embrace the light that softly falls.
The sacred whispers through the night,
Guiding us toward the light.

Flow like water, bend like the tree,
In the currents, find your plea.
The sacred dance of ebb and tide,
In this flow, let hope abide.

Look within, and you will find,
The universe, wholly aligned.
Surrender now, and let it be,
In the flow, we find the free.

The Rebirth of the Spirit's Promise

From ashes rise the heart anew,
Awakened by a love so true.
In the dawn, the spirit sings,
A song of hope, of new beginnings.

The old must fade, make way for light,
In the chrysalis, the soul takes flight.
With every tear, a seed is sown,
In faith, the spirit's strength has grown.

In the quiet, the heart reborn,
Welcomes the light of the early morn.
A promise kept, through trials faced,
In the embrace of love, we're graced.

Dance in the joy of life's embrace,
Feel the warmth of the sacred space.
With every heartbeat, rise and sing,
To the beauty this rebirth brings.

In the garden of the soul divine,
Nurtured by love, the spirit shines.
Trust the journey, hold it tight,
For in rebirth, we find our light.

Beneath the Sacred Canopy

Under the branches, ancient and wise,
Whispers echo in the skies.
With every rustle, nature's hymn,
Invites our hearts to trust within.

In this haven, souls take flight,
Guided by the soft, sweet light.
Beneath the leaves, spirits blend,
In the sacred bond, we transcend.

The canopy shelters all in need,
With roots entwined, together we feed.
From the earth to the heavens above,
In harmony, we find our love.

Here in the shadows, peace resides,
Washing away the worldly tides.
In unity, hearts begin to see,
The sacred flow of divinity.

Gathered in grace, we stand as one,
In the glow of moon, beneath the sun.
With every breath, life's purpose known,
Under the canopy, we are home.

The Journey of the Soul's Embrace

Life's road unfolds with every step,
In the journey, love adept.
With every turn, the spirit knows,
In grace, the heart forever grows.

Through valleys low and mountains high,
Each spirit sings a sacred sigh.
In laughter's light and sorrow's rain,
The soul embraces joy and pain.

Guided by the stars above,
The journey finds its core in love.
In shadows deep, the light will shine,
Through every phase, the soul divine.

With every heartbeat, truth revealed,
In every challenge, love is healed.
The journey wears its sacred face,
In every step, the soul's embrace.

As the sun sets and dawn appears,
The path ahead dispels our fears.
Embrace the journey, let it flow,
For in the love, our spirits grow.

Unraveling Threads of Hope

In the tapestry of grace, we find our way,
Each thread a whisper, guiding night and day.
Bound by faith's embrace, we rise and soar,
In every heart, a light forevermore.

When shadows loom, and doubts begin to spread,
Courage blooms gently, where angels tread.
Hope is the fire that warms the chill of dark,
A beacon shining bright, igniting the spark.

Through trials we wander, in search of the dawn,
With every step taken, new strength is drawn.
United in love, we stitch our dreams tight,
Together we stand, in the sacred light.

Threads of compassion weave stories untold,
A fabric of mercy, strong and bold.
In sorrow and joy, we intertwine,
For in every heart, the divine shall shine.

So let us gather and cherish the thread,
For in unity's bond, there's nothing we dread.
We unravel our fears in the warmth of hope,
With faith as our guide, together we cope.

Beneath the Wings of the Sacred

Beneath the wings of the sacred we dwell,
In reverence, we listen, hearts compelled.
With every prayer whispered into the night,
We find our strength in the softest light.

Angels surround us, their presence we feel,
In moments of silence, our spirits heal.
Guided by love, we traverse the skies,
The essence of grace in our fervent cries.

We dance with the stars, each dream a prayer,
In the warmth of intention, we gather and share.
The sacred embraces, lifting us high,
Together we rise, like birds on the fly.

Beneath the wings, our burdens are light,
In harmony's song, our souls take flight.
Trusting the journey, as seasons unfold,
In every heartbeat, the divine is told.

So let us gather beneath heaven's dome,
With faith as our shelter, we find our home.
In the wings of the sacred, we find our bliss,
A chorus of hope in each loving kiss.

The Symphony of Inner Peace

In the stillness of night, a symphony plays,
Woven with whispers and soft, gentle rays.
Melodies echo in the depths of our soul,
As we dance in the silence, becoming whole.

With every heartbeat, the rhythm unfolds,
A harmony tender, and love untold.
In breaths that are calm, we discover our grace,
As we seek the divine in a sacred space.

The notes of compassion rise high in the air,
Uniting our spirits, dissolving despair.
In the embrace of stillness, layers unwind,
Revealing the treasures that dwell in the mind.

Through trials and laughter, our symphony grows,
A tapestry vibrant, where compassion flows.
In harmony's embrace, we find our release,
A pathway to wisdom, our journey to peace.

So let us listen to the song of the heart,
With each note a blessing, we play our part.
In the symphony shared, we rise and rejoice,
For in unity's music, we hear our own voice.

The Labyrinth of Love

In the labyrinth of love, we wander and weave,
Each turn a reflection of what we believe.
With every soft whisper, devotion ignites,
Leading us deeper through heart's sacred sights.

The walls of our worries begin to dissolve,
In the embrace of compassion, we find resolve.
Guided by kindness, we travel the maze,
In the dance of our spirits, a luminous blaze.

With hands joined together, we traverse the night,
In the warmth of connection, our souls take flight.
The journey of love is both simple and grand,
A sacred adventure, a map drawn by hand.

Through laughter and tears, our path intertwines,
Each step in this labyrinth, a sign that aligns.
In the depths of our souls, the truth comes alive,
A love that awakens, equipped to survive.

So let us embrace this intricate dance,
In the labyrinth of love, we take our chance.
With hearts open wide, we will boldly tread,
For in every heartbeat, the divine is fed.

Illuminated by the Divine Whisper

In silence, I hear the gentle call,
A flicker of light, breaking the fall.
The breath of wisdom, softly bestowed,
Guides my spirit on this sacred road.

With every moment, grace does weave,
Threads of love for which I believe.
The whispers dance in the morning dew,
Each word a blessing, tender and true.

In shadows deep, the light does gleam,
Illuminating every hidden dream.
My heart awakens, a flame ignites,
In the arms of faith, I find new sights.

The stars above, a celestial choir,
Singing of mercy, quenching desire.
As I wander through this sacred space,
I feel the touch of eternal grace.

Let love be the guide in darkest night,
With each step forward, I seek the light.
For in the journey, divinity's near,
Each whisper a promise, daily and clear.

The Sacred Tapestry Within

Threads of faith entwined with care,
Woven stories, beyond compare.
Each knot a lesson, memories blend,
In the tapestry of life, we mend.

Colors bright, from pain and joy,
Interwoven patterns no time can destroy.
The weaver's hands, though tired and worn,
Craft masterpieces, eternally reborn.

In stillness, the heart can discern,
Love's gentle touch, a soft, warm burn.
Deep within, the sacred springs flow,
Nurturing seeds of hope, we sow.

Each thread a prayer, each weave a song,
In unity's arms, we all belong.
Together we rise, together we stand,
In the sacredness of this promised land.

Embrace the light that forever glows,
In the tapestry of love, it shows.
The higher purpose, the sacred plan,
Unites us all, each woman and man.

Journey Through the Valley of Light

In the valley where shadows fade,
The sunlight warms, the fears invade.
I walk with hope, each step defined,
In the embrace of grace, I find.

Mountains rise, the path does twist,
Yet faith is stronger than any mist.
With every breath, I feel the lift,
A journey blessed, a precious gift.

Streams of mercy flow nearby,
Whispering secrets, as clouds drift by.
In valleys deep, the soul explores,
The light within, forever soars.

With open heart, I seek and find,
In every tear, a love entwined.
The valley's lesson, time cannot erase,
In the warmth of light, we find our place.

Through trials faced, our spirits gleam,
Embracing all, we rise and dream.
For in this journey, we gain our sight,
Illuminated in the valley of light.

The Opening of the Heart's Door

Knock, and the love shall be revealed,
The heart's true treasures are concealed.
When fear subsides and courage reigns,
The opening path, where hope remains.

With every prayer, I sense the grace,
In the quiet moments, a sacred space.
The heart's door opens, gently wide,
Inviting peace to dwell inside.

In vulnerability, strength is found,
A symphony of love that knows no bound.
Each heartbeat echoes, a sacred song,
In unity, our spirits belong.

Light floods in, banishing strife,
Transforming shadows, breathing life.
As the heart blooms, it shines and soars,
In the embrace of love, forevermore.

Open my heart to the world outside,
Let compassion flow, and fears subside.
In this sacred act, we all unite,
The opening of hearts brings forth the light.

The Essence of Divine Devotion

In silence, hearts reach high,
Prayers rising, like smoke to the sky.
In every breath, a sacred sigh,
The essence of love, our spirits rely.

With hands clasped tight, we gather near,
In faith's embrace, we cast out fear.
Through trials faced, our path is clear,
Divine devotion, forever sincere.

Each moment shines with holy grace,
In humble hearts, we seek His face.
Ward off darkness, find our place,
In eternal light, we find solace.

Songs of praise fill the air,
In every note, love's perfect care.
Through every sorrow, a whispered prayer,
The essence of our souls laid bare.

Together we stand, hand in hand,
In unity, a promised land.
Through trials and joys, forever we'll band,
Our hearts ablaze, like flames so grand.

Eternal Whispers Beneath the Stars

Beneath the stars, we softly pray,
In the night's embrace, our fears give way.
Whispers of love, in shadows sway,
Eternal echoes, guiding our day.

Each star a hope, cast in the night,
A gentle reminder of divine light.
In silence deep, our spirits take flight,
Eternal whispers, pure and bright.

Nature speaks in sighs and breeze,
In moonlit calm, our souls find ease.
Through sacred paths, our hearts appease,
In every corner, the cosmos we seize.

With every dawn, blessings unfold,
Stories of faith, timeless and bold.
In gentle light, our truths behold,
In eternal whispers, love's grace retold.

United as one, our spirits ascend,
In the realm of stars, the heart can mend.
Bound by the cosmos, our paths we'll blend,
Eternal whispers, our dreams transcend.

The Arbor of Inner Peace

In the arbor green, shadows play,
Branches swaying, light's gentle ray.
In stillness found, we find our way,
Inner peace blooms, come what may.

The heart a garden, tending with care,
Roots planted deep, in truths we share.
Each moment cherished, a sacred prayer,
In the arbor's arms, love's gentle glare.

Birds sing sweet, in harmony rise,
Nature's chorus lifts to the skies.
In every leaf, a tale survives,
The arbor of peace, where spirit thrives.

Through storms that rage, we learn to bend,
In unity's strength, hearts will mend.
A path of grace, our voices blend,
In this sacred space, there's no end.

Together we grow, side by side,
In the embrace of love, we confide.
Under the arbor, our hopes reside,
Inner peace, our faithful guide.

Echoes of Grace Through Time

In whispers soft, the echoes call,
Like gentle waves, they rise and fall.
Through ages past, we stand tall,
Grace leads us on, embracing all.

In sacred moments, we recall,
The lessons learned, through love's enthrall.
Every heartbeat, a timeless thrall,
Echoes of grace, our spirits enthrall.

Through trials faced, we learn to weave,
In threads of faith, our hearts believe.
Each step forward, a chance to cleave,
Echoes of grace, in love we receive.

In every sunset, a story spun,
In the dance of light, our lives begun.
Guided by stars, in peace we run,
Echoes of grace, forever one.

Together in spirit, our voices rise,
In harmonious love, we touch the skies.
Through the tapestry of time, wisdom ties,
Echoes of grace, in every sigh.

Where Spirit and Heart Converge

In the stillness of night, faith gleams bright,
Where whispers of love take gentle flight.
A sacred path woven through the stars,
Embracing the light that heals our scars.

In prayer, the heart finds its way home,
To realms where eternal spirits roam.
Boundless peace in every heartbeat's call,
In communion with the Divine, we stand tall.

Each tear shed, a blessing beautifully clear,
In sorrow, the soul learns to persevere.
With open hearts, we gather in grace,
For in unity, we find our place.

Beneath the heavens, our spirits align,
In moments of silence, the stars shine.
Together we rise, unbroken and free,
Where spirit and heart weave eternity.

Let love guide us through the tumult and strife,
For in every struggle, we discover life.
With faith as our lantern, we journey on,
In the dance of creation, we are reborn.

Threads Woven by Celestial Hands

In the loom of creation, threads intertwine,
Celestial hands craft a design so divine.
Each moment a stitch in the fabric of grace,
Together we weave our sacred place.

With every heartbeat, a story unfolds,
In whispers of love, the universe holds.
Guided by stars, we dance through the night,
In the warmth of hope, we find our light.

With threads of forgiveness, we mend and renew,
In the tapestry of life, we find strength to pursue.
Through trials and joys, we gather each hue,
Our spirits entwined, eternally true.

Each life a pattern, uniquely designed,
In the grand masterpiece, our hearts are aligned.
Together we flourish, together we grow,
In the embrace of love, the Spirit flows.

As we weave our stories, be gentle and kind,
For every encounter, a purpose we find.
In the sacred threads, we are never apart,
Woven by hands of the Divine, in our heart.

In Search of Divine Resonance

In the quiet of dawn, whispers of grace,
Echo through valleys, time's sacred space.
Each breath a question, each heartbeat a prayer,
In search of the love that's always there.

Through shadow and light, the Spirit does guide,
A compass of hope, forever allied.
With open hearts seeking the sacred sound,
In silence and stillness, the truth will be found.

Where the waters flow deep, we listen and yearn,
For the wisdom of ages, the lessons we learn.
In the dance of existence, we sway side by side,
In the circle of life, our spirits abide.

Finding beauty in struggle, the fire that molds,
In the love that we give, a story unfolds.
Each moment a chime in the symphony vast,
In the harmony of faith, we are ever steadfast.

With every step taken on this sacred quest,
We journey through trials, knowing we're blessed.
In search of Divine, One beats as our heart,
Resonance eternal, never to part.

The Beat of Eternity's Gift

In the silence of night, I hear a soft drum,
The beat of eternity calls me to come.
A rhythm of grace flows through my veins,
In every heartbeat, love still remains.

In the light of the morn, the echoes resound,
Each pulse a testament, sacred and profound.
Together we move to the dance of the skies,
In the embrace of the Spirit, the soul never lies.

The heartbeat of nature whispers wisdom untold,
With every breath taken, a secret unfolds.
In stillness and chaos, the truth we can hear,
For in every heartbeat, the Divine draws near.

Through laughter and tears, we walk hand in hand,
In the pulse of existence, together we stand.
With faith as our rhythm, we rise and we fall,
In the beat of eternity, we are one and all.

As cycles of time weave love's perfect plan,
In the heart of creation, we find where we can.
With hope in our hearts, we cherish this lift,
Together we sing, the beat of eternity's gift.

The Luminous Threads of Existence

In the weave of time, so divine,
Each thread a story, each life a sign.
Bound by love, we rise and blend,
Together in light, where shadows end.

In the stillness, whispers flow,
Guiding our hearts to seeds we sow.
Radiant spirits, we intertwine,
Crafting a tapestry, pure and fine.

Through trials faced and lessons learned,
In every heartbeat, a flame is burned.
Unity sings in the fabric's grace,
Embracing the warmth of the sacred space.

The stars above, a compass bright,
Illuminating paths in the night.
As one we journey, souls aglow,
Through the luminous threads, we shall grow.

Merging of stories, old and new,
A symphony sung in every hue.
In each embrace, divine love calls,
In this existence, the spirit enthralls.

A Holy Quest for Inner Truth

In quiet moments, still and pure,
We seek the path, the heart's allure.
With every breath, a step we take,
Toward the light, the soul's awake.

Mountains rise, and valleys spread,
In search of wisdom, we are led.
Through doubt and faith, we find our way,
In shadows of night, we greet the day.

Voices echo in the silent night,
Guiding our spirits to take flight.
With open hearts, we embrace the quest,
In the realm of truth, we find our rest.

In sacred texts, the answers lie,
The universe's truth, we cannot deny.
With humble hearts, we seek and learn,
For inner light, our spirits yearn.

With vision clear, we rise above,
Connected to all, wrapped in love.
In this holy quest, we unite as one,
Journeying forth 'til the race is run.

The Sacred Rhythm of Being

In the pulse of life, a sacred beat,
Every heart echoing, intertwining meet.
With each kind word, a melody plays,
A symphony of grace, in endless ways.

Nature whispers in rhythms divine,
Guiding our souls in a sacred line.
With every sunrise, the world ignites,
In harmony's dance, our spirit delights.

Through the storms, we find our way,
The rhythm of being shall not sway.
In trust, we surrender to the flow,
Within each moment, the truth shall grow.

As the rivers run and the seasons turn,
In gratitude, our spirits learn.
In the sacred rhythm, we are one,
Underneath the moon, beneath the sun.

In unity, we tread this sacred ground,
Where love and light forever abound.
The heart's true music, forever we share,
In the sacred rhythm, we find our prayer.

Embracing Grace in Every Step

With tender steps, we walk this path,
Embracing grace, we find our laugh.
Through trials faced, we rise anew,
In each moment, the divine breaks through.

With open hearts and arms outspread,
We greet each day, where angels tread.
In the beauty of life, we find our song,
A dance of love, where we belong.

In kindness' gaze, we see the light,
Embracing shadows, we ignite the night.
With every breath, we choose to see,
The grace in moments, wild and free.

Through every stumble, in every tear,
We rise with courage, casting fear.
Hand in hand, our spirits soar,
In the embrace of grace, forevermore.

With faith as our guide, we walk the way,
In each small act, love will convey.
Through weaving hope in every part,
Embracing grace, we open the heart.

Whispers of the Divine

In silence, hear the sacred call,
Each heartbeat guides, we heed the thrall.
The sky unfolds a tapestry bright,
And stars proclaim His boundless might.

Through trials faced, our spirits rise,
With faith we walk, beneath the skies.
His light ignites the darkest night,
In every shadow, shines the right.

In whispers soft, His presence near,
A gentle balm that calms our fear.
In prayerful hearts, the truth ignites,
We find our peace in sacred rites.

With every tear, a lesson learned,
In love's embrace, our hearts are turned.
The grace of God, a fountain flows,
In humble hearts, His mercy grows.

So let us walk this path of light,
With open souls, prepared for flight.
To realms above, where angels sing,
In unity, our praises ring.

Echoes of the Soul's Journey

In valleys low, our spirits roam,
To seek the truth, to find our home.
Each step we take is heaven's grace,
A pilgrimage to love's embrace.

Through every sorrow, every tear,
The echoes of our prayers draw near.
In unity, we rise and shine,
Our souls connect, the divine line.

With hope as light, we wander free,
In sacred space, we come to be.
The journey wide, with paths unknown,
Yet every heart is never alone.

As seasons change and time moves on,
The silent songs of faith are drawn.
In whispered dreams, we seek the way,
A beacon bright, to guide our stay.

So let the journey be our song,
In harmony, we all belong.
With every breath, we feel the call,
The echoes of the One in all.

In the Garden of Grace

In fragrant blooms, the Spirit grows,
A garden filled with love that flows.
With every petal, blessings spread,
In quiet moments, all is said.

Beneath the boughs, we find our rest,
In gentle arms, we are so blessed.
The presence soft as morning dew,
In every glance, a vision true.

We tend the soil with faith and care,
In every heart, His love we share.
With joyful hands, we sow the light,
In kindness warm, our souls take flight.

In prayerful whispers, seeds are sown,
The garden thrives as love is grown.
With every season, we shall reap,
In gratitude, our hearts will keep.

So let us wander, hand in hand,
Through sacred trails, in faith we stand.
In this garden, forever free,
United in love, just you and me.

Where the Spirit Rises

In realms above, the spirit flies,
Where love abounds and fear denies.
The wings of grace, they lift us high,
To touch the stars, to reach the sky.

In every heartbeat, whispers flow,
Inviting faith to spark and grow.
A gentle breeze, the Spirit's guide,
In endless hope, we choose to ride.

Through trials faced, we find our voice,
In trust we stand, in faith we rejoice.
With open hearts, we share the light,
In harmony, our spirits bright.

In sacred moments, we align,
With all creation, pure and divine.
Where love transcends, our souls ignite,
In unity, we claim the right.

So let us rise, on wings of grace,
In every breath, we find our place.
Together soar, where spirits sing,
Embracing all the joy He brings.

Illuminated Pathways of Grace

In dawn's soft glow, we find our way,
With faith as guide, we shall not stray.
Each step a prayer, each breath a song,
In love and light, where we belong.

Through valleys deep, where shadows fall,
His hand extends, we heed the call.
Beneath the stars, our spirits soar,
In grace divine, forevermore.

The whispers of truth in winds that blow,
With hearts aglow, our spirits grow.
A journey blessed, with trials faced,
In every tear, a hope embraced.

As rivers flow, so too we share,
The light of Christ, a truth laid bare.
In kindness found, His love entwined,
We walk the path of the humankind.

So let us tread, with joy and peace,
On sacred ground, our souls release.
In every smile, a sweet refrain,
Together bound, we break the chain.

The Sacrament of Self-Discovery

In quiet moments, we turn within,
To find the place where we begin.
With gentle eyes, we seek the light,
A sacred dance, in day and night.

The mirror shows our hidden grace,
A soul unveiled in sacred space.
Through trials faced, the heart expands,
In love's embrace, with open hands.

Each whisper soft, a guiding star,
Reminds us who we truly are.
In silence kept, the truth unfolds,
A treasure found, as life beholds.

With every step, the journey grows,
Revealing depths where wisdom flows.
In faith we trust, our spirits rise,
To see the world through loving eyes.

The sacrament of self we find,
A dance of heart, a fate entwined.
In this great journey, we discern,
The sacred flame, forever burn.

Unveiling the Heart's Hidden Sanctuary

In stillness deep, the heart resides,
A sacred space where love abides.
With every breath, we come to know,
The inner light, a gentle glow.

As petals soft, our souls unfold,
Revealing truths, both warm and bold.
In quiet grace, the veil gives way,
To show the path of light today.

Through trials faced, our spirits sing,
In moments sweet, the joy they bring.
As shadows fall, the light will shine,
In every heart, a glimpse divine.

Each tear we shed, a story told,
Of lessons learned, of love retold.
With open hearts, we seek to see,
The hidden gifts that set us free.

So let us journey, hand in hand,
To unveil wonders, vast and grand.
In unity, we find our peace,
In every heart, the sweet release.

Seraphic Light in the Midst of Shadows

When darkness falls, we lift our eyes,
To seek the light that never dies.
In hope restored, our spirits rise,
With faith adorned, we touch the skies.

The seraphs sing in twilight's glow,
Their melodies, a gentle flow.
In times of strife, their whispers clear,
Remind our hearts that love is near.

Through trials faced, the soul ignites,
In every fear, the spark invites.
With courage found, we walk the night,
And find our way by inner light.

In shadows cast, the truth unveiled,
A love that lives, that never failed.
With every step, we rise above,
In seraphic glow, we find pure love.

So let us stand with hearts aligned,
In unity, our souls combined.
For in the dark, the light will gleam,
An endless hope, a sacred dream.

Milton Keynes UK
Ingram Content Group UK Ltd.
UKHW020038271124
451585UK00012B/930